MW00465375

Coachable

9 Essential Elements of Basketball,
Excellence and a Strong Faith

Colin T. Stevens

ISBN 978-1-64515-199-9 (paperback)
ISBN 978-1-64515-200-2 (digital)

Copyright © 2019 by Colin T. Stevens

All rights reserved. No part of this publication may be reproduced, distributed, or transmitted in any form or by any means, including photocopying, recording, or other electronic or mechanical methods without the prior written permission of the publisher. For permission requests, solicit the publisher via the address below.

Christian Faith Publishing, Inc.
832 Park Avenue
Meadville, PA 16335
www.christianfaithpublishing.com

Printed in the United States of America

Average players want to be left alone.
Good players want to be coached. Great
players want to be told the truth.

—Doc Rivers

Acknowledgments

I am grateful for many things in life, but the people who have influenced me stand at the top of what I'm grateful for.

Thanks Mom and Dad, for raising me in a way to believe in myself, to be kind to others, and to go after my dreams. I'm so grateful for you two because we all know that you can't choose your parents, and I've got the best.

So many coaches have influenced me along the way in my playing career and in my coaching—training career. I appreciate the ones who gave me a shot, pushed me and believed in me. There's a handful of those guys, and you know who you are. So thank you! I also appreciate the coaches who cut me, didn't believe in me, and pushed me to the side. If it weren't for you all, I may not have known how much I really love this game and believe in myself. So thank you.

And to my wife Laura, thank you for believing in me, especially when things have been difficult and low. And thank you for soaring with me when things have been great and light and awesome. I couldn't have asked for a better lifelong teammate!

Finally, to my Lord and Savior and Friend, Jesus Christ. You have displayed what it means to live this life fully connected to God the Father. And thank you, God, for your unrelenting coaching of me. Thank you for pushing me and molding me. Thank you for the grace that you give me that keeps me close to you. I will be eternally grateful for your love.

Introduction

B asketball is a game I have loved since I was a youngster. I was decently gifted athletically, so I played nearly every sport as a kid. But this game quickly separated itself in my heart as the one I loved. One of the things I loved about it is that I could play without anyone else. I just needed a ball and a hoop, and I could play for hours. As I grew older I realized that I'd have to practice a lot to get better. Although I had God-given gifts with speed and athleticism, the gift of good size was not in God's plan for me. So I'd have to outwork everyone else, if I was going to be any good. I made good grades, kept my nose clean, and worked hard in high school. We had a very good coach, and he helped turn around what had been a historically poor program into a conference championship team in my senior year. I will add that we had some really good players on that team. It was some of the most fun I ever had with the game.

But I still struggled. I wanted to play in college, and at an eye-popping 5'7" I wasn't exactly getting the attention that I wanted. And it wasn't just my height. I wasn't anything flashy. I could shoot and score, but I was much more of a traditional point guard who led the team and facilitated before I looked to attack. It's funny as I write this now...I was so confused on why I wasn't getting recruited back then. I just didn't get it. I was even player of the year in my conference my senior year. But as I look at my high school self with the perspective that I have now, I totally get it. Hindsight is truly 20/20.

So without any scholarship offers on the table, I chose to go to Towson University with the idea of walking on to the team. It turns out I didn't do enough research, and the head coach at the time wasn't very interested in keeping walk-ons. I would get one try-out and then a phone call the next day wishing me luck on the next part of my basketball career. That next chapter was intramurals. I was crushed. It was the first time in eight years that I wasn't playing on a legit team. It made it even harder when everyone that I played against in intramurals or pick-up asked me why I wasn't playing somewhere. This was a tough and humbling season of my life. I believed I could play at the college level even division one, but it seemed like I was the only one who believed that. My faith was tested here. My faith in my ability and my faith in God's plan for me. I was certain that God had given me the ability and the passion to do more in basketball, but at this point it wasn't making sense.

Fast forward a bit and some DIII coaches started calling me after the winter break while I was still enrolled at Towson. One of those coaches was the late Dave Manzer. Dave was the head coach at Messiah College in Pennsylvania. He began to recruit me, and we developed a cool relationship. We talked about hoops, our families, and we talked about God. He made it clear to me that he was looking for a basketball leader and player who would lead the team spiritually too. I was honored by his belief that I could do that for his team. I was honored but also a little foolish. Although no DI programs had shown any interest in me even as a walk-on, I still believed I could play at that level. I explained that to Coach Manzer, and in his graceful way he understood. But not only did he understand, he continued to put forth effort to help me. He spoke to his dear friend about me trying out for his team. He was very close with Pete Strickland who was a third-year head coach at Coastal Carolina University just outside of Myrtle Beach, South Carolina, eight hours south of Baltimore where I was from. I connected with Coach Strickland, and I went down to visit the school and meet with him. Coach seemed like a good guy, but he was honest with me. He told me he hoped that I like the campus and the school because if I came down and didn't make the team, then I'd just be a regular student. It sounded a little risky but heck, it was a shot and I felt like I was finally going to get a fair look from a coach at the level I wanted to play at.

And so I made the leap. I enrolled in the fall semester of 2002 at Coastal and began working out in preparation for tryouts. To make a long story short, Coach Strickland kept four walk-ons, and I was the last one of them. Thirteen scholarship guys and the four guys who made the team made seventeen players, and I was number 17. But I made the team! I was so excited just to put on the practice gear. I was just pumped to be a part of the team. But I could not have planned what would happen next. I was the third string point guard, which basically meant I wasn't even going to get any scout team minutes in practice. But in the preseason our starting point guard got hurt. Then six games into the season, our next point guard got injured and both of these guys were out for the season. In about a month I went from seventeenth man to starting point guard, more by default than anything. I started twenty games that season and went on to earn a scholarship for my final two years. We had a coaching change in my senior year that was really tough on me because I was so fond of Pete Strickland for giving me a chance and believing in me. But I'm also thankful that I was able to learn from Buzz Peterson and his staff who pushed me to a new level in my senior year.

I am now into my fourth year as a high school varsity head coach. And over the past nine years, I have been building my own player development company where I have worked with youngsters all the way up to NBA players and everything in between. We have several coaches and trainers that work for our company in different areas of the country. I look back and think of the coaches that impacted me in my career, and it makes me think of what impact players that I work with will get from me and the coaches I work alongside.

And let's keep it real—the best coach we'll ever have is our God. If we let him, he'll train us, correct us, encourage, and mold us into the men and women…the coaches that he desires us to be.

We, as coaches, know that our jobs are incredibly demanding and challenging. In our day in time, you are expected to win at any level. If you don't win, you're out. But here's the deal; there is so much more to coaching than winning. And winning is very important. That's why we compete and play the game. But if we're going to be special coaches, then we have to define ourselves differently than the world and the media does. Hopefully this compilation of coaching strategy and an inward look at the heart will help all of us be different in a way that makes a deeper impact on our players.

Chapter 1

What Makes a Great Defense?

Offense sells tickets. Defense wins championships.

—Paul "Bear" Bryant

Bear Bryant was onto something here. And it's never been more true in the game of basketball as it is in today's game. Offense sells tickets, gets notoriety even gets the biggest contracts in the NBA. But it's always been said that defense wins championships. And as coaches that is what we are most interested in. So we must understand, study, and implement what makes up a great defense. I believe there are five components that the best defensive teams all have in common.

1) They are committed and emphasize defense on an everyday basis.
   - Teams that only focus on defense occasionally will have breakdowns and let downs often.
   - The coach keeps the bar high for what is acceptable effort, focus, communication, and energy for the team.
   - It's the players, the leaders on the team, who have to hold each other accountable. This may cause some yelling or arguing at times, but in the right environment, this is healthy communication to keep the standards high. In a poor environment, yelling and arguing is a recipe for disaster.

2) Each player is committed to being the best defender they can be.
   - The coach can emphasize defense all he or she wants. The team can practice it day in and day out, but if the players aren't putting their best effort forward

into becoming the best defender they can be, then there will be holes and weak links in the defense.

3) Players defend for the team, not just for themselves.
   ➤ We see this in great defensive teams. They are phenomenal at help-side defense, rotating after defensive breakdowns, and contesting every shot attempt. They don't just defend and guard their man; they all take it personally if the team gets scored on. It's a "WE" mentality.

4) They do the little things all the time.
   ➤ They box out each possession. If they can't get to their man, they hit a man.
   ➤ They pursue 50/50 balls at all costs. They don't assume someone else will get it.
   ➤ They communicate constantly and consistently. The whole team understands terminology, and each player uses it to keep the whole team on the same page.

> They will sacrifice their body for the good of the team. They'll take charges, dive for loose balls, and jump into the stands in the pursuit of a loose ball.

5) Good offense leads to good defense.
> When these great defensive teams get the shots they want on offense, it allows them to get their defense set and lock down. But when teams take poor shots, rushed shots, and turn the ball over, then they are not able to set their defense. They have to play in scramble mode. So these great defensive teams are often well disciplined on offense too because good and timely offense allows them to consistently be outstanding on the defensive end.

Great defensive teams hold true to these five components year in and year out because the coaching staff has created that culture. Great defensive teams will find themselves competing in every game because they make it difficult on their opponent.

Now the question is…how can we be great defenders in life? So much about the game parallels to our day to day living off the court. There is no doubt that we have an opponent, but how can we have a great defense? Let's get into the word and see what God has to say about it.

In Ephesians 6:12 we are told that "our struggle is not against flesh and blood but against the rulers, authorities, powers of this dark world, and spiritual forces of evil in the heavenly realms." Okay, so if our struggle is against stuff we cannot see, how do we defend against it? How can we conquer it?

The rest of the passage in Ephesians 6:13–18 goes on to say, "therefore, put on the full armor of God so that when the day of evil comes, you may be able to stand your ground; and after you have done everything, to stand. Stand firm then with the belt of truth buckled around your waist, with the breastplate of righteousness in place, and with your feet fitted with the readiness that comes from the Gospel of peace. In addition to all this, take up the shield of faith with which you can extinguish all the flaming arrows of the evil one. Take the helmet of salvation and the sword of the Spirit, which is the word of God. And pray in the Spirit on all occasions with all kinds of prayers and requests. With this in mind, be alert and always keep on praying for all the saints."

So then let's break this down to see what Paul (the author of Ephesians) is saying and how we can be great defenders.

1) To recognize that our struggle is not against flesh and blood but against the spiritual forces of evil in the heavenly realms.

   ➤ It is massively important we understand that our enemy is unseen. The enemy is not flesh and blood...this means the enemy is not our teacher or our boss or our co-workers. And until we recognize this and practice against our true enemy, we will continue to be defeated in battle.

2) Practice your defense day in and day out... "Put on the full armor of God."

   ➤ We have to practice! Day in and day out we need to put on TRUTH and RIGHTEOUSNESS, and be ready with PEACE. We must have FAITH, and know that as Christians we are living with SALVATION. Of these things we must be reminded on a daily basis.

3) Good offense leads to good defense…"Take up the sword of the Spirit."

> Can you imagine being in the *Braveheart* battle scenes or in the *Lord of the Rings* battles…and you have no sword? You have no way to attack and be on the offensive against the enemy? This would be a terrifying place to be. We must get into the Bible which is the "Sword of the Spirit" so we can attack back at our enemy. Without a sword we are dunzo.

4) Communicate…"Pray in the Spirit on all occasions."

> Good teams communicate. We need to pray to our Father in heaven on all occasions with all kinds of prayers and requests. We need to talk with God regularly. We need to be in communication with our coach so we can defend well.

5) Defend for the team…"Keep on praying for all the saints."

> Good teams don't just communicate, they communicate with each other

and for each other. Prayer is powerful, and it's huge for us to pray for our brothers as this is a way we can help them defend their hearts and minds. We also need to encourage and uplift our brothers and sisters in truth. The world throws lies at us one after the other, and it's so important that we help our team stay locked into the truth of who we are and whose team we are on!

Great teams defend well. And great defenses have high expectations. Let us have high expectations in defending for our team and for each other. And may we honor God with our effort each day with our defense on the court and in life.

Coach's Keys

Our struggle is not against flesh and blood but against the rulers of this dark world.

Put on the full armor of God day in and day out. Get in his Word and connect with God through prayer.

Remember that you have a team of fellow warriors. You are not in this battle alone.

Chapter 2

Know Your Role

The strength of the team is each individual member.
The strength of each member is the team.

—Phil Jackson

Every successful team from the corporate world to the family and definitely in team sports has members that understand what their role is and what they contribute to the team. But then the question arises…*How does someone know what his/her role is?*

So how do basketball players know what their role is on the team? This information has to be doled out by the coach, the leader of the organization. The coach has to see the big picture and how the puzzle pieces fit together in order to have each team member play his or her role so that the team has the best chance to succeed. By no means is this an easy task. The coach and the staff should put a lot of time into discussing and communicating roles to the team. They need to truthfully understand player's strengths and weaknesses and be able to help the player see what the coaches are seeing.

Now if roles are not defined, this can and will be a big issue for the team. Here are some problems your squad might run into if roles are not clearly defined and accepted.

1) *Everyone tries to get theirs.* Let's face it. We live in a world where statistics are glorified and spread across social media. In my day it was awesome to get a picture and your name in the paper. Nowadays, players are getting tweeted about every day! If players don't understand their role for the team, they will likely do whatever it takes to get pumped out on twitter and Instagram, and that causes players to try to score the most points or do something crazy just to get some love on social media. Not everyone

on the team is a great scorer, and players need to know and accept that.

2) *The team takes a back seat.* If roles are not clearly defined, then each player is really only thinking about themselves. How much playing time did I get? How many points did I score? How many assists did I have? What was my full stat line? Players need to understand that they are on a TEAM, and the success of the team is why they are there. They may really enjoy the game, but if they are not willing to contribute to the success of the team, then they should seek out an individual sport like golf or tennis. Each player on the team has to put the success of the team as the highest priority.

3) *Players are confused.* Without a clearly defined role, players will not understand what is expected of them. Confusion leads to players being unable to contribute their best effort. When players have to think too much about what they are doing it will lead to hesitation and often sloppy or wild play. If the players don't know what the coach is expecting from them or they don't know what the team needs from them, they will

often miss the mark and get off course. They'll likely be dissatisfied because they don't know why they aren't playing as much or how they are supposed to contribute. This is especially the case for some practice players or players who only see a few minutes per game. Their attitude on the bench and in the locker room will severely affect the team whether it be positively or negatively. But if they know their role and put the team first, then they'll know what's expected and how they can help the team.

And really when we are talking about roles, we are talking about what gifts a player has. Some players are natural athletes—fast, strong, quick, and they can jump well. Some players may lack athleticism but have great IQ and skill. Others may be more naturally gifted on the defensive end. While others may not have many physical gifts at all but can contribute to the team with great energy and a great attitude. A good coach will figure out how to define roles for players based upon their gifts and communicate to them in a way where the players buy in. A good coach will also understand that things may change, and there are many things coming in a season that are unforeseen. And they may need to help players adjust their roles accordingly.

For the past couple of years, I have coached a very skilled player who is a great ball handler and great shooter. He is our best scorer and best all-around player. In a game last season, he was hesitant to shoot the ball on several occasions. During a time-out I asked him, "What are you doing? Why aren't you shooting?" In hindsight, I think he may have been struggling with confidence a bit or distracted by other things that were happening in his life, and he may have been a bit checked out in that game. After I pulled him to the side and asked him what was going on, he kind of had a blank stare and said, "I don't know." So I reminded him sternly of what his role for our team was. This got him back on track, and he had a solid second half and was more aggressive in looking to score.

And as coaches, we are often reminding our players of this: "You're our best rebounder! Get in there and do what we need you to do! As our point guard, we don't need you to shoot every time. Run our sets and make sure everyone is on the same page." Coaching is constantly reminding players to stay the course for the team. To stay within their lane.

So the coach leads the charge on making sure everyone understands the part they need to play for the team. Now it's on the players to accept that role and not only to accept that role but to excel in that role.

This can be a difficult task at times as I mentioned before. So many players just want to get the glory. It's important for players to feel needed. When they feel needed, they will take ownership of their role and desire to excel in that role for the team. The worst thing a coach can do is just focus on a few of the best players on the team and ignore the other players. A great way to get players to buy into their role is to praise them in front of the team for what you've been asking them to do. Players want to feel needed and want to know that they're excelling, so when they are praised for what they've been asked to do, this reinforces the role acceptance.

Again this is one of the greatest challenges as a coach—to have players truly accept and buy in to their role. But a great coach and a great culture can make this happen year in and year out.

And as we transition to how this affects all of us in the bigger picture, we have the parallel that God is our coach. But what roles would he have us play, and how does that apply to us in all areas of our lives?

In First Corinthians, chapter 12, Paul writes to the church of Corinth about Spiritual gifts. I'm assuming some members of the church there are having trouble understanding, defining, and accepting roles within the church. I encourage you to read the full chapter.

> The body is a unit, though it is made up of many parts; and though all its parts are many, they form one body. So it is with Christ. For we were all baptized by one Spirit into one body—whether Jews or Greeks, slave or free—and we were all given the one Spirit to drink.
>
> Now the body is not made up of one part but of many. If the foot should say, "Because I am not a hand, I do not belong to the body," it would not for that reason cease to be part of the body. And if the ear should say, "Because I am not an eye, I do not belong to the body," it would not for that reason cease to be part of the body. If the whole body were an eye, where

would the sense of hearing be? If the whole body were an ear, where would the sense of smell be? But in fact, God has arranged the parts in the body, every one of them, just as he wanted them to be. If they were all one part, where would the body be? As it is, there are many parts but one body. (1 Cor. 12:12–20)

This is big time! We are all looking for our purpose. We all want to know that we are going in the right direction. And for Christians that are a part of the body (team) of Christ, we need to know our role. And when we know our role, then we know how we can truly contribute to the team. When we know our role, then we can live a life full of purpose. Too often we are not excelling in life because we are trying to be something different than what we were intended to be. God has made us an ear, but we are trying to be a hand because it seems cooler, or there is more glory in it. We must know what our gifts are and what we've been called to be and then live that out.

I can help with the general-purpose part for sure. The number one purpose for all people is to live in a daily loving relationship with our God through Jesus Christ. However, as for the role you play in life in the body of Christ, I cannot help you, but your coach can…

Paul goes on to say, "Now you are the body of Christ, and each one of you is a part of it. And in the church, God has appointed first of all, apostles; second, prophets; third, teachers; then workers of miracles, also those having gifts of healing, those able to help others, those with gifts of administration, and those speaking in different kinds of tongues."

Paul is offering what roles and purposes God may have given some of these people. It's almost like Coach K saying, "And some of you will be scorers, rebounders, defensive stoppers, good ball handlers and passers; and others will be great energy guys or even team managers."

God is there to help us, and more importantly he has made each one of us for a purpose. And he's created us to contribute to the team of Christ. He knows us better than we know ourselves.

I bet many will have questions of how you can know what your role is or what your gifts are. This is what I'd say. Ask God to reveal it to you. And if you don't feel like he's responding, ask him again and again and again. He wants us to know clearly about the gifts he's given us so that we can best help the team, and so we can fulfill our purpose on earth. If you still have confusion, I would encourage you to ask your close friends or family about what you're gifted with. They will know. But the coach should still be the one to define it for you.

As I previously stated, it is very important for the coach to define the role for the player. But the next most important is for the player to accept the role. You know what this takes? Honesty. Most players don't accept their role not because they don't like the coach but because they are trying to be something they are not. They may not like what they've been gifted with and wish they had been imparted with something else. I would argue the same for us in the body of Christ. Many times we are unwilling to accept what God has truly gifted us with because we'd rather be something that we are not; something we think is better than what we are. And likely, in our minds, we'd rather be something more recognized, something more glorious. This is where we have to be honest with ourselves and be willing to operate out of our gifts. And sometimes our honesty may need to be accompanied by humility and the understanding that God knows us better than we know ourselves, and he knows how we will best operate and fulfill our purpose.

Just like we need our players to know, accept, and excel in their role for the team, we also need to know, accept, and excel in our role for the team of Jesus.

Coach's Keys

Make a list of your personal
gifts. Make a list of what
you are not gifted with.

Do you know God's purpose
for you? Are you willing to
accept his role for you?

How do you think you can
most contribute to the success
of the body of Christ?

Chapter 3

What Are You Putting In?

*We are what we repeatedly do. Excellence,
therefore, is not an act but a habit.*

—Aristotle

Great players don't just pop up on the scene nor
do great coaches. There are certain innate quali-
ties that each of us are born with that make us unique
as discussed in the previous topic. However, what
turns an athlete into a great player? Or what turns a
leader into a great coach? It all has to do with what
they put in, what they consume on the regular.

1) *Time.* Great players put in countless hours in the gym. They work on their skills and their fitness. They get in the weight room to work on their strength and endurance. As they develop and grow in their knowledge for the game, they will watch film and study the great ones. Now, players who are seeking greatness don't do this so they can say that they are doing it. They don't do it so they can post it on social media. They don't do it so they can say that they want to be great. They spend countless hours on improving themselves because they truly desire to be great, and they understand probably at an early age that TIME is one thing they must spend with the game. If you truly love something, then you will spend the most nonrenewable resource on it—time.

Great coaches don't start out on the top. It takes years and years for them to become equipped to lead a team and an organization. Many great coaches started out as student managers and weren't great players in their own right. Great coaches will spend countless hours building relationships, truly learning *x*'s and *o*'s, and learning how to manage their players and in-game coaching. Most people will never actually see or appreciate how much time great coaches put into the game—it actually becomes part of who they are, not just what they do. So for all of you, young coaches out there that feel like you should be moving up in the ranks, be patient and keep working on becoming the best you can be. Then you can be ready for your next opportunity.

My last words on the coaching piece regarding time is the coaches that are truly the best don't waste TIME with worrying about their wins and losses. They feel more accomplished by the relationships they've made and the impact they've had on players. They know it's bigger than just the game or their record. Coaching with winning habits leads to positive results on and off the court.

2) *Nutrition.* Looking back I wish I would have understood this more as a player and taking advantage of the fact that most players don't pay enough attention to it. Food is basically fuel to the body of an athlete. Body=Vehicle. And if we put the wrong fuel into our vehicles, they will run sluggishly and underperform. So often play-

ers don't understand that when they eat poorly this leads to them feeling sluggish and having less energy or even less motivated. I can't stress this enough. What we eat greatly impacts how we feel and how we perform on a regular basis.

My wife and I just really started changing our diet. It's been a gradual process, and she's led the charge on it. But it's almost silly to me that neither one of us paid much attention to it in college when we were playing our sports day in and day out. And now we're both on the cusp of not being as fit and weighing more than we'd like, we've decided to pay more attention to what we are putting in our bodies—and it has made an enormous difference. But how much more for active athletes!

Now I won't get into the details fully about what is good fuel and what is bad fuel as this is not my area of expertise. But I can confidently say this. If it's fried, full of sugar, or processed to stay on the shelf for years, then it's probably gonna slow you down. But if it's from the earth and hasn't touched a processor, then you're good to go. A strong and conditioned colleague of mine says, "If God made it and it comes from the ground, then eat it. It's good for your body."

3) *The Mind/Spirit.* Now we start getting in the real stuff—the heavy, unseen, and most impactful stuff. However, this is also the most overlooked area of consumption. What are we putting into our minds and our spirits on a daily basis?

The problem here is we do not realize that we're actually putting things into our minds. What do I mean by this? Well, we call it watching TV, listening to music, reading on our iPads and Kindles, scrolling through Facebook or Twitter or Instagram or Snapchat or listening to the radio. That's what we call it. But the truth is we should call it feeding our minds.

What we watch, listen to, and read greatly impacts our thoughts and our beliefs. And if you think about it, our thoughts and our beliefs are the most fundamental pieces of our lives. What we believe shapes our world when we look at the big picture, and what we think about on a regular basis shapes how we act and feel on a daily basis. We must protect our thoughts and beliefs.

We're going to dive into the book of Philippians to look at our thought life. In this letter to the church of Philippi, Paul was writing to them from a Roman prison. The church of Philippi had sent a gift to him, and he was writing to them to thank them for the gift and to encourage them to stay strong in the faith. Yes, he was writing from prison and encouraging the free people of Philippi to stay strong in the faith.

> Finally brothers, whatever is true, whatever is noble, whatever is right, whatever is pure, whatever is lovely, whatever is admirable—if anything is excellent or praiseworthy—think about such things. Whatever you have learned or received or heard from me or seen in me—put it into practice. And the God of peace will be with you. (Phil. 4:8–9)

Very simply put…think about good things! This is coming from a man who is currently in prison and has faced imprisonment all over. He could have very easily said, "It's rough in here, guys. The accommodations are poor. I don't get to eat much, and I'm tired of being in prison." And if he wrote that to them, they would have likely empathized with him and understood his position. But he chooses the tougher and higher road. He implores them to think about what is true and noble and right and pure and lovely and admirable. This is a powerful message. He understands that what he decides to focus on and what he decides to think about will greatly impact him on a daily basis, and it will greatly impact those he leads.

And moreover, he tells them to put into practice what they have learned from him or received from him or seen in him. He understands that he sets the tone for the church. If he complains, then they will as well. If he talks bad about so and so, they will do the same. He is fully aware that he is being watched, and he sets an incredible example.

And this is tough for players and coaches, especially when you've been on a losing streak. Well, I've got news for you…Paul has been on a more difficult losing streak than we've ever been. He's been shipwrecked, beaten, malnourished, imprisoned, and barely escaped death, all for the spread of the Gospel. I mean, come on, this guy knows about losing streaks. But he continues to hang on to what is true in the bigger picture. He doesn't feel sorry for himself and get all soft. He chose to think about good things even when he has faced legit life-threatening challenges, and players and coaches want to complain about a losing streak or tough administration. Paul has got to be chuckling in heaven when he sees what we complain about.

Coaches need to take heed of this. You tell your players not to complain to the refs. Well, do you complain to the refs often? Complaining to the refs and talking with the refs are two very different things. You tell your players to spend extra time in the gym to get better. Do you spend extra time in the film room and the gym to improve as a coach? You tell your players if they have good energy and good attitudes, then they will have a better impact on the team and have a chance to get more playing time. But do you display good energy and a good attitude day in and day out, regardless of the circumstance? Your players will be like you and do what you do. We, as coaches, must realize that we set the tone for our group, team, or organization.

In the previous passage, we talked about what we think about. But what about what we believe? What about the bigger picture? This is what Paul wrote to the church in Rome.

> "No, in all these things we are more than conquerors through him who loved us. For I am convinced that neither death nor life, neither angels nor demons, nei-

ther the present nor the future,
nor any powers, neither height
nor depth, nor anything else in
all creation, will be able to separate us from the love of God
that is in Christ Jesus our Lord"
(Romans 8:37–38)

First of all, he says we are MORE than conquerors
through Jesus. Then he says that once we've been on
team Jesus, nothing in all creation can separate us
from the love of God. Those are two firm and powerful beliefs, and if we hang on to those beliefs, they
will shape us in an incredible way.

And we must understand that each day we are
going to be lied to and coaxed into believing something different. You're not good enough, you're too
small, you're too old, you're too not worthy of love.
Can you imagine if we let those beliefs shape us? That
leads to death even while we're living— we'd be dead
and lifeless inside.

Let us put our belief and faith in those two
things that Paul stated. We are more than conquerors. We will not be separated from the love of God.
Let's choose to believe these two truths every day and
see how it shapes us!

Coach's Keys

What are you currently feeding your mind on a daily basis? What are one or two things that should change?

We as coaches set the tone for the energy and attitudes of our organization.

Lock into the truth that we are more than conquerors and we will not be separated from God.

Chapter 4

The Process

*If you run into a wall, don't turn around
and give up. Figure out how to climb it,
go through it, or work around it.*

—Michael Jordan

"The Process" has become very much a buzz-term in our world as of late. You hear it often…"Trust the Process." And although it is a buzz-term, it is also very valid and has plenty of depth to it. So I'd like to unpack this overused term for a little while here and see how it relates to basketball and what God might have to say about it.

The other day as we were doing a meal and message with a high school training group, we asked the players what they thought about the process. We asked them what they actually thought "the process" is. Here's what they had to say.

- The process is about working hard even when you're not getting anything out of it or even when you don't get shout-outs or recognition on twitter.
- The process is about getting better, just a little bit every day.
- Surrounding yourself with people who have been there and following their process.
- Making sacrifices for what you want.
- Keeping your head on straight.
- Being able to deal with the negativity and adversity that's coming.
- Having faith that the process is going to work—keeping the faith when it's hard.

I think they did a pretty good job here, don't you? It really sounds like these players have a decent understanding about what the process is. But let's take it a little deeper.

The process itself is actually about doing what it takes to get to where you want to be. This could be as a player or as a coach or even as a team. This could also be in your career or your marriage. We often dream of how we want things to be, but we often don't take the steps to actually make things how we want them to be. So the process, in a nutshell, means that you will do what it takes to get to where you want to be.

So what does the process take? What are the steps?

1) You have to have a PLAN. And this plan has to have a decent outline of the actual steps you need to take, the relationships you'll need to make, and the ladder you may need to climb to get to where you want to get to.

2) After the plan, you have to consider the COST. What will it cost you to get to where you want to be? This could be countless unnoticed hours in the gym, weight room, or film room. This could be a master's degree, or it could even be serving as an assistant coach for an unknown amount of years before you get your shot at being a head coach. There will be a cost for some-

thing that you want that has value, and you cannot obtain what you desire without paying the price. Many have tried to, but they wind up quitting because they are not willing to fulfill the cost.

3) Lastly, you'll have to MAKE CUTS. And this is where most people falter before achieving their goals. You'll have to make some sacrifices so they you can get to be where you want to be. You'll have to rid yourself of distractions and not give in to the temptation of busyness so that you can stay focused and stay on the path to your destination.

I believe the two hardest cuts everyone has to make are time and relationships.

Time. If you're going to be great at something, then you have to put the majority of your time toward it as we talked about in the previous chapter. If you're more concerned about video games and entertainment than putting in some extra time on your craft, then you can rest assured the process will not work for you. Your time is a nonrenewable resource, meaning you can never get back the time that you've spent doing something. And if you invest it wisely into your craft, then you will keep moving forward.

Relationships. If you're going to be outstanding at anything, you'll have to be different. In fact, to be outstanding means that you "stand out," which is the opposite of "fit in." We are often so concerned about what other people are thinking about us that we don't appreciate standing out and being different. Most of us want to be accepted and to fit in. But if you fit in with the mediocre…Well, I rest my case. There will be some possible several relationships you'll need to cut in order to reach your goal, if it's lofty enough. I would encourage you to keep the ones who love you and challenge you and cut the ones who help you fit in and make you feel good all the time.

So there are three basic steps to the process. But just because the steps are basic does not mean it will be easy. In fact, it will be difficult, it should be difficult. Many times the process is abandoned in the most difficult times. People will say, "I didn't sign up for this" or "I didn't think it would be this hard." But if we will fight through the challenges, no matter how long they may last and we trust the original plan and keep the faith, then we'll be strong and proud on the other side where we end up. It seems like these high school hoopers had it figured out. Although it's easier said than done.

So, what is God's process with us? This process is based on the premise that God wants us to become more like him as was displayed in Jesus his son...as stated in Leviticus 11:44, "I am the LORD your God, consecrate yourselves and be holy because I am holy." God wants us to be like him. So how can we be more like him? What does his process entail? We'll find some answers in John.

> I am the true vine, and my Father is the gardener. He cuts off every branch in me that bears no fruit while every branch that does bear fruit, he prunes so that it will be even more fruitful. You are already clean because of the word I have spoken to you. Remain in me, and I will remain in you. No branch can bear fruit by itself; it must remain in the vine. Neither can you bear fruit unless you remain in me.
>
> I am the vine; you are the branches. If a man remains in me and I in him, he will bear much fruit; apart from me you can

do nothing. If anyone does not remain in me, he is like a branch that is thrown away and withers; such branches are picked up, thrown into the fire and burned. If you remain in me and my words remain in you, ask whatever you wish, and it will be given to you. This is to my Father's glory, that you bear much fruit, showing yourselves to be my disciples. (John 15:1–8)

In this chapter, Jesus is talking to his disciples, and this is one of his famous parables. He is relating us to branches on a tree, or as he says the *true vine*. Here are the steps to the process that jump out at me.

1) "If a man remains in me and I in him, he will bear much fruit; apart from me you can do nothing."

Jesus is saying that we must stay connected to him; he is our source of life just as the source of life for any branch is the trunk of the tree. A branch that is not connected to the tree cannot bear fruit. We must be connected to him constantly. This means we need to be reading the Word and in prayer with him each day, throughout the day.

> 2) "He cuts off every branch in me that bears no fruit while every branch that does bear fruit he prunes so that it will be even more fruitful."

First, he says if we are not bearing fruit, then we will be cut off. This is a strong statement but a beautiful truth. I don't know much about gardening, but I do know that when there is a withered branch that is dying or producing no fruit, it actually takes away from the whole tree. Ever had a player who has such a poor attitude that it actually brings the team down? Well God says he will remove this branch so that the tree can produce more fruit.

The other point here is God prunes or cleans the branches that bear fruit so that they will be more fruitful. This is where we struggle. We think that God should leave us alone when we are doing well, but he wants us to do great…to be holy. So he cleans us and prunes us. This is a bit painful, but it makes us better in the end. We have to trust God's process and allow him to prune us to make us more like him.

There is so much more to be unpacked here, but I think these two points sum up what God wants to do with us. He wants us to remain in him, and if we do remain in him, we will produce fruit that shows we are connected to him. What is the fruit? The fruit is the evidence that God's spirit dwells within us— that evidence is explained in the fruits of the Spirit in Galatians, chapter 5.

My prayer for you and I is that we allow God to do what he wants with us and we will trust his process in making us holy like his son.

Coach's Keys

How do you deal with the difficult times in the process? Do you lean on God?

What cuts could you make with regards to time and relationships that will help you move toward your goal?

What fruit are you currently producing? Do you remain connected to the true *vine* every day?

Chapter 5

Team-First Mentality versus Me-First Mentality

Good teams become great ones when the members trust each other enough to surrender the me for the we.

—Phil Jackson

As coaches we preach to our players that the team comes first. You win with the team, and you lose with the team. This is a team sport, and it is imperative that everyone works toward the success of the team, coaches included. We live in a day-in age where the team is not truly elevated, particularly from outside the locker room—it's the individual players that are most highly glorified in our society today. Of course, the team would not be any good without good players or a good coach. But it's the best teams that get these highly glorified players and highly glorified coaches to put the team first. So let's unpack this "Team First-Mentality versus Me-First Mentality" regarding players and coaches.

Players with a team-first mentality:

1) *Will work to improve themselves.* They come early and stay late to work on their skills and study film to improve their knowledge of the game. They are coachable and look for opportunities to take their game up a notch. This makes them better, and better players make a better team.

2) *Get excited for the success of their teammates.* They know that when their teammates are getting better and garnering success, it likely means more success for the team. They'll cheer them on even if they are on the bench and don't get much personal credit that particular game. They like seeing their teammates do well.

3) *Accept their role and excel in their role.* They are willing to look at the team as one unit

and accept how they can best help the team. Then they will look to thrive in that role and be the best scorer, rebounder, defender, cheerleader they can be. This is a tough one. As I stated before, individual players are glorified more now than ever. And for a player to lock in and accept their role, especially if it means less glory, is tough—but the team-first players will do it.

Players with a me-first mentality:

1) *Don't work to improve themselves.* They won't spend extra time in the gym as they are likely more concerned with their social life or other things that don't require as much work and effort. These players aren't worried about elevating the team by elevating themselves.

2) *Point fingers and place blame.* They don't get excited for their teammates because they're jealous of the attention their teammates are getting. They blame teammates for missed shots or looking them off. These players don't take responsibility for their own actions or lack of action—they'd

much rather talk about what everyone else is doing wrong, especially the coach. These players cause factions in the team because of the trash they talk about other players or coaches.

3) *Have a bad attitude or poor body language.* They are so stuck on themselves that they can't see that they are dragging the team down with their negativity. If they aren't getting what they want, you can see it all over their face and so can the rest of the team. These guys are sitting down on the bench when the rest of the team is up, cheering their teammates on. These guys don't give high fives to teammates or won't extend a hand for a positive touch. They are self-absorbed, and they aren't thinking about the success of the team; they are concerned with what they are getting.

The best teams have players that are onboard with team success. This doesn't mean that players don't have individual success; in fact, the best teams actually have players that stand out more because the team is better and made up of better pieces. When the team functions as one, then all the parts of the team look better. Now it's up to the coaches to culti-vate that culture and enforce the team-first mentality. Coaches with a team-first mentality:

1) *Develop a culture and hold true to it.* They set their standards and expectations of the players, and they enforce it with conse-quences. When it comes to the culture of the team, there is no difference between star player and bench players. They all must be held to the same standard. This promotes respect within the team. Now, each player is different, and coaches will have different relationships with different players. But as far as discipline and expectations go and as soon as the coach lets the star players get away with things that are deemed unac-ceptable to everyone else is the time that team loses its culture.

2) *Put the extra work in.* These coaches will study film and learn more about the game. They will study their opponents and be prepared for what's coming. They will con-nect with other coaches and ask questions and opinions in order to keep learning and growing. They understand that if they want

their players to keep getting better, then they themselves must keep getting better.

3) *They care about the growth of the team.* They put the health and growth of the team above wins and losses. This means they may kick a player off the team, regardless of talent level, because they are making the team unhealthy. This means they will play difficult competition in order to truly test and challenge their team even if losses are the outcome. These coaches will take time after practice to talk with players and connect with players. Players will know that this coach cares about them outside of the lines.

Coaches with a me-first mentality:

1) *Put winning over everything.* They believe that winning defines them as a coach. In this case I'm not talking about the professional level. At professional level, coaches are largely defined by their W/L record. But even at the highest level, these coaches with the best teams have a great culture and keep high standards within the orga-

nization. This goes for college coaches as well. People want to say that college athletics are amateur, but in every sense, D1 athletics that generate revenue for the institution are a business. And the coaches of those teams are CEOs, and if the team is not winning for consecutive seasons, then they will be on the hot seat. So how can they not put winning over everything? The best coaches understand that you develop a culture, you hold true to it and work hard, and then good things will come. Maybe not at first but good things will come eventually. Coaches with a me-first mentality just want to win now, at any cost. So they won't discipline their star players, in fear of upsetting them. They won't play a challenging schedule, in fear of losing games. These coaches will create a selfish culture. After all, the team will take on the personality of the coach.

2) *Point fingers and place blame.* They don't take responsibility for what's happening with the team. They will blame players, and they will blame assistant coaches for breakdowns or poor play or bad scouting. These

coaches will look for every reason to say, "It wasn't my fault." This will create a sense of paranoia on the coaching staff and fostering distrust within the locker room. Rest assured, this organization is going south.

3) *Don't care about the success of others.* They are unwilling to help coaches or players advance in their careers. They won't use their network to help others reach their goals because they are too concerned about reaching their own. What these coaches don't understand is that the more success the players and coaches have that are under you, the better you look as a coach. So if these coaches would get their heads out of the sand and help some people, they'd actually be helping themselves. It's all about perspective.

The coaches I have had in mind as I write this segment have been Gregg Popovich, Steve Kerr, Brad Stevens, Coach K, John Calipari, Buzz Peterson, Pete Strickland, Ed Conroy, and a handful of high school coaches that really go about things in the right way. You may not agree with how coaches do it, but coaches that create team-first cultures also seem to reach the highest levels of success, and maintain it. When coaches get things backward, it comes out as winning is the only important part, and they don't force their players to go through the process of what makes winning with a team sustainable.

It's easy to get things backward. Most of the time we are praised on the results we get, not for the work it took to get the results. And what if we are doing the right things as coaches—putting the team first and creating a culture that does so, but we still aren't getting the desired results?

In Matthew 6:33 as Jesus is smack dab in the middle of his "Sermon on the Mount," he tells the crowd that is gathered on the mountainside, "But seek first his kingdom and his righteousness, and all these things will be given to you as well."

Earlier on, in this passage, he is talking about how people worry about what their life will be like. What they will eat or drink and what they will wear. He is telling them about how people get so caught up in the things of this world and how they get focused on them and exclusively look to satisfy their worldly needs and wants. He's telling them that they are too focused on winning.

In verse 31 he says, "So do not worry saying, 'What shall we eat?' or 'What shall we drink?' or

'What shall we wear?' For the pagans run after all these things, and your heavenly father knows that you need them." He's telling them, "Look, I get it. You need water and food, you need to clothe yourselves. But everyone needs these things. Even people that have no faith need these things. But you are different, and because you are different…" "Seek first his kingdom and his righteousness, and all these things will be given to you as well." He's telling them, if you get consumed with the things of this world, then you will lose perspective. The first priority for all of us should be to seek his kingdom first. And if you'll notice at the end of verse 33 he tells us that "all these things will be given to you as well." Meaning, after we seek his kingdom and his righteousness, we're still going to get the things that we need. He will provide for us. And if we seek him first, we'll be more concerned with the kingdom (team first), then we would be if we were just consuming the things of this world (me first).

After reading this in my quiet time the other day, I realized that I often get this backward. I seek first the things of this world, hoping to check off the boxes, get the bills paid, and try to get ahead in life. But when I do it this way, God has shown me that I'm just like the coach that puts winning above everything else and is not concerned enough about the culture and the process of making a lasting and winning team. I lose perspective on what truly matters, and I don't remain disciplined to the standards that I truly believe in. I will make compromises in my heart and mind that shouldn't be made. I will drift away from him.

What he calls us to as men and women and coaches of God is to seek first his kingdom. And he will give us our process, and he will lead our culture. And then we will be able to honor him and lead our coaching life with an *eternal* perspective. And he says that all of the other things we need will be taken care of as well. And what we prioritize or what we put first will make all of the difference in our life whether it be in our relationships or our career. If we trust him, we will seek his kingdom and his righteousness first.

"Lord, it is my prayer that we would seek you first each and every day, regardless of how busy and chaotic our days get. I pray that we would ask you to lead us and our organizations and families in a way that honors you, and that we would trust your work that says that you will take care of our every need. Teach us how to create a team-first mentality in our teams and in our homes, and may you receive ultimate glory for our wins and successes. Amen."

Coach's Keys

Where are your priorities as a
coach? List your top five.

Do you trust that God will fulfill
your needs? Or is that something
you will always take upon yourself?

We must seek him first
and let him guide our path
on and off the court.

Chapter 6

Scouting Report

*A quick way for any player to
make himself better is to think about what
he himself doesn't like to play against.*

—Bobby Knight

The goal of a coach is to bring the members of
the team together to play and compete at their
highest level as one unit to win the game. There is
so much a coach can do to prepare his/her team
for the contest. They will spend countless hours in
the gym, behind the scenes, work in the film room,
and daily efforts of maintaining a high level of team

moral. But something we haven't touched on much at all yet is the opponent. And there is no contest, no competition without an opponent. In chapter one, we defined that our battle is not against flesh and blood…but now we get to be a bit more specific. Bringing us to this: One of the most important parts of being prepared for the game is to have a detailed scouting report.

A scouting report is a compiled study of the other team. A good scouting report will include:

1) What their tendencies are on offense and on defense.
2) A breakdown of impactful players on their team.
3) What their strengths and weakness are as a team and an individual basis.
4) A scouting report will reveal how the other team wants to play, and it will also come with a plan on how our team can take them out of what they want to do. A plan on how our team can control the game.

A scouting report is all about preparation. You want to be able to know your opponent so that you can defeat them. The worst thing that can happen to the coach that is providing a scouting report is for them to be surprised by a player who was not mentioned as an impactful player on the report.

In one of my college games years ago when I played for Coastal Carolina University, we played a nonconference opponent in December. In the first half, they had a player that came off the bench and hit a three-pointer. Not a big deal right? He wasn't on our scouting report that we reviewed prior to the game. Well, it became a big deal when he went on to hit six three-pointers that game, and we lost. I remember our head coach snapping his neck looking at the assistant coach who prepared the scouting report. Every time this kid hit a three, our assistant coach shrank on the inside.

I can laugh about it now, but in competition it is the worst thing to be caught off guard, to be unprepared, and to not know what your opponent is going to come at you with. Scouting reports are massively important if we want to become a consistent winning team with preparation as part of our culture. We must know our opponent.

So let's dig a little bit. What opponent do we face day in and day out? Many of us would say our boss feels like our opponent. Sometimes it feels like our spouse is on the other team. At times it may feel like a teacher or a peer is trying to hold us back, and they are the opponent.

But as we have reviewed before, in Ephesians 6:12 Paul reminds the church of Ephesus, "For our struggle is not against flesh and blood but against the rulers, against the authorities, against the powers of this dark world, and against the spiritual forces of evil in the heavenly realms."

To put this more simply in basketball terms, Satan is the coach of a team of evil spirts, and their goal is to take us out. Satan failed when he tried to overthrow heaven, and he was cast to the earth and out of the presence of God. There were angels that sided with him in his revolt on God, and they too were banished from heaven. Ever since then, Satan has been attacking those whom God loves—his creation, his sons and daughters. It is imperative that we understand that we have an opponent that looks to take us out, to keep us separated from God. That is how he wins. Our sin is what separated us from God in the first place as we were born with it, thanks to Adam and Eve. Christ came to reconnect us to the father through his death and resurrection. If Satan can keep us separated from God, then he wins.

So let's look at what a scouting report might be on our spiritual opponent.

1) "He was a murderer from the beginning, not holding to the truth, for there is no truth in him. When he lies he speaks his native language, for he is a liar and the father of lies" (John 8:44). Christ explains to us that he is the ultimate deceiver and will lie to us as a part of his nature. How often do we believe the lie that: if we have more wins, then we'll be more significant; if we have more money, cars, and clothes, then we are better than others that don't; if our marriage is hard, then we should quit because it should be easy; or we should try to fill our emptiness with sex, drugs, alcohol, attention and things of the like. We will be lied to day in and day out constantly. And we must be aware of the tactics of our evil opponent if we want to stay connected to God our father.

2) "For Satan himself masquerades as an angel of light. It is not surprising then if his servants masquerade as servants of righteousness. Their end will be what their actions

deserve" (1 Cor. 11:14–15). Here, Paul is explaining to the church of Corinth that Satan will disguise himself as an angel of light. Evil disguising itself as good. How many times have you and I sought after something that we thought was good but turned out to be evil? This happens when we are not in tune with God, and we seek something that he does not intend for us to have. But we must understand that some of this come from the sin in us and much of it comes from the great deceiver. We must be wary and test all things to see if they are truly good. We have to be connected to our God daily, hourly, in order to guard our hearts against the enemy.

3) "Do not conform any longer to the pattern of this world but be transformed by the renewing of your mind. Then you will be able to test and approve what God's will is—his good, pleasing, and perfect will" (Romans 12:2). It is so important that we understand Satan was cast out of heaven to earth, and he now runs amuck on this planet. It pleases him for us to be confused on what we think and who we serve. His

goal is to get us to think that this world is all there is and for us to be consumed by it, for us to be consumed by our pride and self-interest. He wants us to be just like him. But in this passage in Romans, Paul commands the church in Rome to "conform no longer to the pattern of this world but be transformed by the renewing of your mind." Renewing happens often, not just once. Renewing means continual growth and refreshing. We must renew our minds with the Word of God so we can stand against the devil and his schemes. We cannot follow the pattern of this world and please God. The line has been drawn, and we must choose our side.

So we've got to know our scout on the opponent. We've got to know when he is going to attack us and how he's going to attack us. I mean, we won't know all the time when it's him. But if we're connected to God, then his Holy Spirit that lives in us will be sounding the alarm when Satan and his team attacks.

So my question is…Do you know when you are most vulnerable to attack? This isn't rocket science.

For a very interesting perspective on how and when Satan may attack us, I encourage you to read *The Screw Tape Letters* by C.S. Lewis. This is a brilliant fictional book from the perspective of a demon that Satan has assigned to take out a particular human. It's an eye-opening, enjoyable, and cunning—read all—together.

Over time and seeking truth, I've learned that this is when I'm most vulnerable to the lies and temptations of the evil one.

1) *When I'm tired and burnt out.* "Fatigue makes cowards of us all"—the great Vince Lombardi once said, and isn't this the truth? It's like when I'm tired, I just don't have the fight to put up a fight. I'll give in. I'll eat that extra dessert. I'll watch that stupid show. I'll let my guard down. I'll conform to the pattern of this world. Satan knows that if he can get me to believe the lie that busier means better, then I'll stay on the go and I'll get fatigued. And then he'll strike with temptation.

2) *When I'm not plugged into pursuing God.* I pursue God through time in his Word each day, time in prayer, and once or twice a

week I meet with a group of men who hold me accountable to pursuing him. And I do the same for them. When I am not plugged into these things, then I am a sitting duck. It's tough because in the moment I don't truly know it. And this is where my fellow warriors come in. When I meet with them each week, they can help me see where my weak spots are and help shield me from attack. I believe these weekly meetings have been the most influential in terms of my growth in Jesus in the past five years.

3) *When the unexpected hits.* I recently tore my Achilles tendon playing basketball after some training sessions. I was ticked off. A million thoughts were running through my head; none of which were positive. So many questions. Anger. Frustration. Regret. It all hit at once! And I was a mental mess. If I didn't have a wife and awesome co-workers to speak truth to me and point me toward God, then I would have stayed in that mental mess of confusion and lies for quite some time.

Look, the attacks are coming. I can't tell you that if you do a clean seven-step process, then you'll never fall victim to Satan's schemes. But I will tell you that if you look at Jesus's life often and try to be more like him, then Satan and his punks will have a much more difficult time taking you down and conforming you to this world.

I often get stuck in the middle of trying to please the world and please God, and that just leads me into confusion. If I can stick to one plan, one way, his way, then I can make my stand for God and his kingdom. God implores us to stick with his game plan so that we can stay connected to him and carry out his purpose for us on this earth. That is winning as a Christian.

"O God, will you help us to be aware of our opponent so that we won't be deceived and led astray from you. Help us to renew our minds often with your truth so that we can live in your presence and love. May your truth overpower the lies of the evil one, and may your truth set us free from the lies that we've believed about you and ourselves in the past. Amen."

Coach's Keys

 Satan is the father of lies.
And those lies are what he
throws at us each day.

 Do you know when you are
vulnerable to attack from
the evil one? How can you
be ready to fend him off?

 We need to be aware of ourselves
and our weaknesses. Our
opponent surely is. Then we need
to continually ask God to reveal
his strength in our weaknesses.

Chapter 7

Focus

Lack of direction, not lack of time, is the problem. We all have twenty-four hour days.

—Zig Ziglar

One of the great enemies of excellence is distraction. We as humans can achieve nothing great without a healthy dose of pure, unadulterated, and inspired…FOCUS. And the same goes for our teams, on and off the court. Every team will be hit with distraction. In the basketball world these days, most distractions come from social media and things outside of the locker room. As coaches, we will deal with players being distracted by parents and friends, all who likely mean well, but are not inside the huddle with us and don't have anything at stake with our team.

Focus seems to be a lost art. Now, more than ever, we are pulled in so many different directions. And so are today's youth. Most of them have unlimited access to this huge world via the internet and social media. And though I'm all for advances in technology, I don't believe all of it is good. I think we need to be teaching students how to manage social media, how to say NO to things on social media. Not everything is good for us to see just because there is no censorship. But an unsupervised teen would not know that. In fact, most teens think they know everything anyway so why not take a look at this page or that page? They don't know that what seems mildly harmless at the time can very much lead down a very corruptive rabbit whole whether it's pornography, violence, or just foolish stuff that turns the mind into unproductive mush.

Nearly 80 percent of my on-court worktime has to do with running training sessions for high school, college, and professional players. It blows my mind seeing how many of them will get a brief break for water, then sit down for a minute, then pick up their phone out of habit. This is a loss of focus. What these players see on their phone can absolutely take their minds elsewhere, certainly off what we've been working on the court. They may get a troubling text from family or information about a girlfriend or any news on social media—while these things are not bad in themselves, they certainly take away from what you are trying to accomplish as a team or even in an individual workout.

So here's the truth, focus is a compilation of these things, and these things are hard to come by:

1) *Time.* It takes time to focus. You've got to get your mind centered on the right thing, and you put your mental energy into that. If you get unfocused, it takes time to get refocused. And time is absolutely precious and irreplaceable. Bad teams waste time. Good teams value time.

2) *Effort.* When you are focused, you put your effort toward one thing, one goal. Wasted effort leads to fatigue, and fatigue will ultimately lead to a loss of focus. When players are in really good physical condition, it allows them to focus longer and point their effort in the proper direction.

3) *Discipline.* To be focused on one thing means that you say NO to other things. And those other things that you're saying NO to may not be bad or harmful, it's just that they don't contribute to the goal of the focus. We must be able to say NO to distractions.

4) *Cooperation.* The challenge of a coach is to get all players focused on the same thing at the same time. With all of the distractions that kids face today, keeping players honed in on a team-first mentality will help them stay focused more. Great teams have leaders that help bring other players back to the team focus.

One of the greatest challenges of a coach is to get players to focus on one common goal for the team. Not all players are the same, and some have an easier time focusing than others. Here are some issues that coaches will face.

➢ Players are trying to do too much individually.

➢ Players are getting into one-on-one battles with other players.

➢ Players are worried about their own stats.
➢ Players are worried about what their parents or friends will say after the game.

Let's face it. We live in a world of ever-present distractions and a society that pushes individuality more than it emphasizes unity and collective pursuit. Both distractions and individuality can be the downfall of any team. A great team will be full of focused individuals who combine all of their gifts and abilities to one common focus of being the best team they can be. As coaches, here are some things we can do to help our teams stay unified and focused.

1) *Remove distractions.* Close the doors and make it a team-only practice. You can also make sure that cell phones are left in the locker room.
2) *Make sure the focus is clear.* Tell the team what you're trying to achieve in the practice or give them a focus that they can lock into and then give them feedback on how they're keeping up with the focus.
3) *Give them a curfew.* I think this only works if they actually believe in the team goal. You can micromanage every player, but

that will drive you and your players nuts! I think if each player buys into the team goal and they understand the importance of their rest (or just staying out of trouble), then they are likely to adhere to the plan. If they aren't bought into the team goal, it doesn't really matter what rules you institute, they'll still be focused on themselves and what they want.

4) *Share with them.* Talk to them about stories of players and teams of the past becoming distracted from their goals and tell them about the result of their actions. Young people get really connected with stories, especially if it involves players they really look up to. Stories and connection go a long way into helping players stay focused.

5) *Give them consequences.* This is really the only way that players can understand that there is a "cause and effect" to the decisions they make. If you've made a rule that no cell phones are allowed in practice or in the locker room during game time, then you have to have a consequence if this is breached. If they break curfew, then there must be a consequence. Consequences

help us all to take ownership of our actions. And consequences also tell young people who need guidance that you as the coach are not full of hot air. That you are committed to the team goal as well, and that discipline is needed for the team to achieve its goals.

It is very difficult to keep young men and women focused these days. Unlimited access to information on the internet whether good and bad and the rampant craze of social media make it even more difficult. But it is vastly important that we teach our young people. That's what it means to coach. Don't get so enamored with winning that you fail to teach your players how to be great people. And we have some help. As we look into the word, we can see what our heavenly coach would tell us about staying focused.

It's almost easier to set our goals in the basketball world. We want to win games as a team; we want to win a championship; players want to have great stats, receive a scholarship, or go pro. When we know our goal, then we can set our focus. But how about in the spiritual world—the true foundation of who we are as people? What does God say our goals should be? If we can uncover these goals, then we can truly lock in and focus.

1) "Be imitators of God" (Eph. 5:1).
2) "Do not conform any longer to the pattern of this world but be transformed by the renewing of your mind" (Rom. 12:2)
3) "Do not be yoked together with unbelievers. For what do righteousness and wickedness have in common? Or what fellowship can light have with darkness" (2 Cor. 6:14)?
4) "Dear friends, since God so loved us, we also ought to love one another" (1 John 4:11).
5) "Come near to God and he will come near you" (James 4:8).

And this is just a few of the things in the new testament that we are encouraged to strive for. Sheesh! My head is spinning. How can I do all of these things? And if I read the Bible on a daily basis, I'm probably going to find many more things I should be shooting for. It almost feels too daunting, like in order for me to keep up with all of these things, then I need to be a perfect person. It can feel overwhelming.

Well, did you ever think that your team might be overwhelmed? Like you just keep throwing stuff at them, and there are actually too many things for them to try to keep up with? If there are too many goals or things that you're trying to emphasize, then it makes it really difficult to focus—and sometimes that just leads to giving up.

Well, I think God knows this about us. Being the original engineer of the human body, mind and soul, he knows we can be overwhelmed and out of sorts. He also knows we'll be plagued by doubt and discouragement…more arrows from the enemy. But thankfully he knows us. And so he simplifies it for us. And from the very lips of the Son of God we are given two goals,

"Love the Lord your God with all your heart and with all your soul and with all your mind." This is the first and greatest commandment. And the second is: "Love your neighbor as yourself." (Matt. 22:37–39).

So if we can love God with all of our being, then we are achieving the goal. (I'm chuckling as I write this. Like, yeah, let's just go ahead and do that. That's easy…) But at least, we have something to shoot for. Love our God with all that we are. If that's the goal, then we need to be focused. We need to lock in. But how do we lock in? Here are some helpful ways we can stay focused on loving our God:

1) *Spend time with him.* To love someone, you must know someone; and to know them, you must spend time with them alone where you can get to know their heart and they can know your heart. I don't believe that Jesus says, "Love the Lord your God…" in a way like we "love" a celebrity, an infatuation kind of love but with no connection. No, our God wants us to KNOW him and love Him. And Jesus shows us this as he often left his disciples and the crowds to go spend time with God in prayer. Alone. In the quiet. You see, I think many of us think that prayer has to be head bowed, at a certain time of day or meal, and we have to follow this rule and that rule. But prayer is our way of talking to the father and hopefully listening as well. When you love someone, you communicate with them…daily, maybe even hourly. In truth, the more you talk with that someone, the more connected and in sync you will be. Doesn't that sound good? To be in sync with our heavenly father.

2) *Spend time with those who love him.* He calls us to fellowship with one another. Why? Because we will be influenced by who we hang out with. Now, in no way I am promoting "holy huddles," where you group up with some other Christians and never let anyone else in, or you don't associate with those that are not in the church. We are not called to that, and that does not honor God because he's on a mission to get to the hearts of those that are not connected to him, and we are an instrument of his mission. But it is greatly important that we spend significant time with those who love our God in truth, those who know God, and those who will challenge us to keep growing closer to him. We all go in the same direction as those around us. And if we often engage with people who are climbing the mountain on a path that leads closer to God, then that will help us stay on that path. And the adverse is true. If we are spending all of our time with people that are in no way walking toward God and pursuing him, then we'll be on the same path with them too.

3) *Spend time worshiping him.* As much time as we spend worshiping athletes, movie stars, business moguls and musical icons, we should really check ourselves here. And by worship I mean praise, exalt, and spend countless hours talking about your favorite player, rap artist, actor or singer. You see, we were created to worship. But we were created to worship the one who is truly worthy of being praised day in and day out, not for putting a basketball in a hoop or scoring a touchdown—but for creating a beautiful earth and giving life to us. God alone deserves most worship and praise and discussion and water-cooler talk. Let me put it this way for us basketball people. It's like LeBron James just had a 30–15–15 game last night, but we're going to talk about a guy in the G-League who had three points and two rebounds in fifteen minutes of play. You get the idea? There's absolutely no comparison to how great our God is and how great a human can be. How many of these people we idolize heal blind people? Make the crippled walk? Turn water into wine? Raise someone from the dead after

three days? I mean come on, it's not even close. But we've traded worshiping the true KING for worshiping idols, things that are less and are man-made. And yes, athletes, movie stars, business moguls, and musical icons are man-made. We made the arena where all of these things take place, and we made the measuring stick on what determines their greatness. Now please understand, I'm not saying we shouldn't pursue greatness ourselves in any of these given fields; but what I'm saying is when we spend so much time worshiping the things of this world, we won't have much time to worship the only one who is truly worthy.

So if our goal is to love the Lord our God with all of our heart and soul and mind and to love our neighbor as ourselves, then we must be warned of the distractions that can take us off of our *focus*.

The acts of the sinful nature are obvious: sexual immorality, impurity and debauchery; idolatry and witchcraft; hatred, discord, jealousy, fits of rage, selfish

ambition, dissensions, factions
and envy; drunkenness, orgies,
and the like. I warn you, as I did
before, that those who live like
this will not inherit the kingdom
of God. (Gal. 5:19–22)

I like how Paul tells the Galatians that these acts of the sinful nature are obvious. I wish we treated these things like they were obvious and that we'd actively resist the things of the sinful nature. I believe that Paul was trying to tell the Galatians that these are the things that take you further from God, so stop doing them. I believe we struggle with the same things today, in the twenty-first century, as the Galatians did in the first century, but in case you may think our world is so different and our actions of sin are not so obvious, this is my attempt to simplify things. Here are a few distractions we deal with on a daily basis that keep us from loving God with our whole being.

1) *The love of money.* "People who want to get rich fall into temptation and a trap and into many foolish and harmful desires that plunge men into ruin and destruction. For *the love of money* is a root of all kinds of

evil. Some people eager for money have wandered from the faith and pierced themselves with many griefs" (1 Tim. 6:9–10).

The LOVE of money is a root of all evil. This was a warning two thousand one hundred years ago, and it's just as relevant today. Our world tells us if we make more money, we will be happier. But the truth is the more money we make, the more stuff we buy. And the more stuff we buy, the more time and energy we have to spend on maintaining our stuff. And to maintain all of that, we need to work more to make more money, *so that we can be happy.* What a nasty cycle we are born into in the western society. The truth is no matter how much money we have, we can be happy, we can live in joy. The people who don't struggle financially aren't the ones with the most money, they are the ones with the fewest financial obligations. As long as our financial obligations outnumber our income, we will always be stressed out about money. But if we decide to love God first and see money just as a tool to be used to benefit the kingdom of God, then we can experience joy in the financial realm. Money itself is not bad at all. It is simply a tool. But "the LOVE of money is a root to all kinds of evil."

2) *The praise of people.* The name of the game in today's western society is... *Who can gain the most attention* in sports, in academics, in comedy. The biggest aim for many people on social media is not to share their lives with their friends, it's to post the quote, picture, or video that will garner the most likes and retweets and shares. We all want something of ours to go "viral"—we want to be known by everyone even if it's just for a quick minute of fame. We think that *"The more followers we have, then the more powerful we are, or the more significant we are".* Well, I want to take a look at what Christ said about aspiring for attention.

Be careful not to do your acts of righteousness before men, to be seen by them. If you do, you will have no reward from your father in heaven. So when you give to the needy, do not announce it with trumpets as the hypocrites do in the synagogues and on the streets, to be honored by men. I tell you the truth. They have received their reward in full. But when you give to the needy, do not let your left hand know what your right hand is doing so that your giving may be in secret. Then your father, who sees what is done in secret, will reward you.

And when you pray, do not be like the hypocrites, for they love to pray standing in the synagogues and on the street corners to be seen by men. I tell you the truth. They have received their reward in full. (Matt. 6:1–5)

This is an awesome punch to the gut of us who are trying to do 'acts of righteousness' so that people see it and give us praise. But what Jesus is getting at is we should do good deeds out of our love for God and let him reward us in his time and in a way that he sees fit. If we do things just to receive praise from men, then that's all we'll get. And what does he call these people? Hypocrites! That is a serious term no one wants to be identified with.

(You can also check out Gal. 1:10 to see what Paul has to say on the matter.)

3) *Busyness.* We are plagued by the idea that if we are busier, then we must be winning or we must be important. And the adverse is often assumed. If we are not busy and running around, then we must be losing or we are unimportant. This is a distraction and a lie.

As Jesus and his disciples were on their way, he came to a village where a woman named Martha opened her home to him. She had a sister called Mary, who sat at the Lord's feet listening to what he said. But Martha was distracted by all the preparations that had to be made. She came to him and asked, 'Lord, don't you care that my sister has left me to do the work by myself? Tell her to help me!'

'Martha, Martha,' the Lord answered, 'You are worried and upset about many things, but only one thing is needed. Mary has chosen what is better, and it

will not be taken away from her.'
(Luke 10:38–41)

Jesus knew about our busyness problem. He knew Martha was awestruck with having him in her house. But Martha was trying to impress Jesus, hoping he'd see everything that she was doing to make his stay special. However, Jesus applauded Mary for seeing that it's more important to spend time with him rather than trying to impress him with her busyness. It is often our busyness that can distract us from what's best. We can all be more intentional with how we use our time.

The most significant thing I've done to combat losing focus on seeking God and keeping in step with his purpose for me is building a daily routine that puts him first. I recently read a book that talked about habits and choices and routines. It rocked me! I have since then set aside an hour in the morning to spend time with God. So now I wake up around five-thirty each morning in order to have time that is specifically dedicated to being connected to him. No email, no social media, no texts. Just me and him. This was a difficult change for me initially as I'm not an early riser naturally. This routine of starting my day with God has made an enormous impact on my walk with him. No matter how crazy my days get, I know I will get refocused each morning with HIM.

Now, I can't stress this enough. My routine is to meet with God each morning. But I don't make my time with him routine. I don't have a task list to check off when I'm quiet with him. I will often spend time listening to worship music on my phone. Sometimes it's fifteen minutes, other times it's an hour. I always have my Bible with me. Sometimes I read a chapter, sometimes three chapters and less time to worship. I spend time in prayer. Sometimes I spend the whole hour walking and talking and listening to God.

The pastor at our church has become a dear friend of mine. And he has been such a valuable mentor in this department. He's helped me understand *how* to pursue God and how to not make it religious routine, but relational refreshment.

So the truth of the matter is our focus needs to be on great things, and the greatest thing we can ever have is a seamless relationship with our God through Jesus Christ and the work of the Holy Spirit in us. My prayer is that we all would put aside the distractions that take us away from what truly matters in this life, and that day in and day out, we can put our attention toward what we are designed for.

Coach's Keys

 Each day we have distractions
thrown at us that are
irrelevant to our goals.

 What things easily take you off of
your focus in seeking God?

 How can you do better at
removing distractions in order
to stay on track or get back
on track toward your goals?

Chapter 8

The Little Things

Success is neither magical nor mysterious.
Success is the natural consequence of consistently
applying the basic fundamentals.

—Jim Rohn

This thought came to me while I was out for a run the other day. Prior to my Achilles injury, I had been putting in some decent effort to get my body in shape, at least in better shape than it has been. I've been going for runs over the past couple of weeks, and I also did some sit-ups after my run. I'm locked into one hundred sit-ups at a time right now.

The thought popped in my head, *You're going to have to do a lot more than one hundred sit-ups if you want to change things!* Then another thought popped in my head and kicked the other one out. This thought said, *If you do one hundred sit-ups today, then it's better than nothing. And if you do one hundred sit-ups for five days a week, then you've done five hundred sit-ups. And if you do that for a full month, then you've done 2,000 sit-ups. And if you do that for a whole year, then...*Well, you get the point.

I'm so thankful for this more positive and truthful thought that dominated the negative thought. It's oftentimes that we push the little things to the side, and we just dwell on the big things. Sometimes what we fail to understand is that it's doing the little things well and often that lead to a better outcome. If I looked to climb a mountain, it's likely that I'd look at the top of it and say to myself, "I want to be there." But the truth is I have to take a step at a time to get to where I want to go, and although this is a bit cliché, I believe as coaches we need to be reminded of this often.

If you are going to have a great team, it's because your team will do the fundamentals well...the little things. Most people on the outside will ask you what players you have and what kind of defense you're going to run, what your offensive style and sets will be. Here's a list of those big things that are actually made up of a bunch of little things.

1) Big Thing = Great Defense
   ➤ Little things that make up great defense:
   a) Pressuring the ball
   b) Being in proper position in help side
   c) Rotating to help the helper
   d) Containing the drive
   e) Being in position to take charges
   f) Matching up in transition
   g) Contesting every shot
   h) Blocking out
   i) Players are in great condition
   j) Finishing the possession with a rebound

2) Big Thing = Great Offense
   ➤ Little things that make up great offense:
   a) There is good pacing.
   b) Timing of sets are in sync.
   c) Ball penetrates the defense with the drive or the pass.

d) Quality shots are taken.

e) The ball advances quickly in transition.

f) Mismatches are exploited.

g) Players understand time and score.

h) Players are skilled.

i) Players are in great condition.

j) The offense flows with movement and passes.

3) Big Thing = Great Team Chemistry
   ➤ Little Things that make up great team chemistry:
      a) Players know and accept their role on the team.
      b) Players trust each other.
      c) Players will sacrifice for the good of the team.
      d) Everyone is aware of who the leaders are.
      e) Players give each other respect.
      f) Players appreciate what each player gives to the team.
      g) Adversity is dealt with collectively.
      h) Players are not in competition with one another for glory.

   i)   Players are in great condition.

   j)   Players work really hard without the sense of entitlement.

Here's an aside...Now you will notice that on *i* in every section of the little things breakdown, I have the same item. Players must be in great shape. Players in poor shape can't play defense for an extended period of time. Players in poor shape will take bad shots and turn the ball over on offense due to fatigue. And players in poor shape will not work hard for the team and won't earn the respect of their teammates regarding team chemistry.

It's easy for us to get caught up in the big things, but if we want to be better in any of these areas as a team, we must focus on the little things day in and day out. Then the big things will take care of themselves. The tough part is our society is a BIG THING society. Most of the time we only see the result of someone's hard work. We don't see the little things that they've been doing to reach their success. We live in the era of highlights. We love seeing the "Big Play" and often get bored with the basic fundamental plays, which actually lead to our desired outcome more than the "Big Play." We want things to come quick and easy. So if we aren't getting what we want out of the work we are putting in, then we often abandon the plan and move on to something else before the original plan even had time to conceive a great result. We must lock in to the little things. Teach and train our players to be consistent, men and women of character, and a part of something bigger than ourselves. But this is the honest truth…players will take on the personality of the coach. And if you want your players to be different, then you may have to look in the mirror and focus on the little things for yourself.

This, however, is not a new concept. In fact, two thousand years ago Jesus taught the crowds he spoke to about the little things.

> Again, it will be like a man going on a journey, who called his servants and entrusted his property to them. To one he gave five talents of money, to another two talents, and to another one talent, each according to his ability. Then he went on his journey. The man who had received the five talents went at once and put his money to work and gained

five more. So also the one with the two talents gained two more. But the man who had received the one talent went off, dug a hole in the ground, and hid his master's money.

After a long time the master of those servants returned and settled accounts with them. The man who had received the five talents brought the other five. 'Master,' he said, 'you entrusted me with five talents. See, I have gained five more.'

His master replied, 'Well done, good and faithful servant! You have been faithful with a few things; I will put you in charge of many things. Come and share your master's happiness!'

The man with the tow talents also came. 'Master,' he said, 'you entrusted me with two talents; see, I have gained two more.'

His master replied, 'Well done, good and faithful servant!

You have been faithful with a few things; I will put you in charge of many things. Come and share your master's happiness!'

Then the man who had received the one talent came. 'Master,' he said, 'I knew that you are a hard man, harvesting where you have not sown and gathering where you have not scattered seed. So I was afraid and went out and hid your talent in the ground. See, here is what belongs to you.'

His master replied, 'You, wicked, lazy servant! So you knew that I harvest where I have not sown and gather where I have not scattered seed? Well then, you should have put my money on deposit with the bankers so that when I returned I would have received it back with interest.

Take the talent from him and give it to the one who has the ten talents. For everyone who has will be given more, and he will have an abundance. Whoever does not have even what he has will be taken from him. And throw that worthless servant outside, into the darkness, where there will be weeping and gnashing of teeth. (Matthew 25:14–30)

In this story Jesus illustrates a couple of things for us.

1) Each man had been given a particular amount of money to handle "according to his ability." The struggle for many of us is we look at what others have and wish we had been given the same thing or even more when it comes to money. The truth is everyone starts life at a different point when it comes to personal economy. Some start with more than they need, and others start with nearly nothing. And there are plenty of us that started somewhere in between. But the "according to his ability" piece here was determined by the master when he was

dishing out the money, not by the servant who was receiving it. I'm sure the master was aware that the servants probably don't see their abilities clearly all the time. And it's not so different with our players. Many times we see them differently as they see themselves. And more times than not, our players see their ability as being well beyond what we see as coaches. This is why we define roles for our players and give them responsibilities based on their ability as determined by the coaching staff, the trusted leaders of the organization. We too must trust that God has given us what we need based upon his understanding of our ability. For we too, like our players, may have a sense of our ability that is off a bit when it comes to what we should be entrusted with.

2) The reward is based upon what we do, not what we started with. Notice, both the first and second servant were invited to share in their master's happiness. He tells each of them on separated occasions, "Well done, good and faithful servant! You have been faithful with a few things; I will put you

in charge of many things. Come and share your master's happiness!" So he's telling us straight up. If you handle the little things well, then I'll give you more. Why would he give us an abundance of responsibility if we can't even handle a few things? So let's ask ourselves...

a) If we want more financial resources—are we honoring God with what we already have? Or do we squander money and live at the top of our means, leaving us little to invest into his kingdom? If we are not honoring him with what we currently have, why would God give us more resources to squander?

b) If we want more friendships—do we handle our few friendships well? Do we love our neighbor as ourselves? If not, why would God give us more relationships to jack up?

c) If we seek a leadership position and more influence—are we handling the mundane part of our jobs well? Are we good with the little things, or do we just push them to the side and hope for a more glorious position? Are we making the best of our current position? If not, how can we be entrusted to lead others?

The point is, it's all about what we do with what we have—not that we need more to do more.

Jesus tells another story in the book of Luke, chapter 16, and he caps the story with this: "Whoever can be trusted with very little can also be trusted with much, and whoever is dishonest with very little will also be dishonest with much." You see, Jesus is telling the crowd it's the little things that make the difference. It's the little things that are the test. So often we give the little things no credit and no recognition because they are not glorious, or they may seem beneath us. But what Jesus is explaining is that the little things are the most critical. If you cannot handle the little things well, handling big things will only be harder.

This truth hits me very hard when it comes to the finances of our home. Like so many Americans, we struggle with debt and the constant temptation to live beyond our means. Our society tells us day in and day out that we need more and more stuff, when it's the stuff that actually enslaves us and in turn, we must work so hard in order to maintain it. This is also true with our relationships and our careers and our families. We need to ask God to help us be great in the little things. For if we can be trusted with very little, then and only then can we be trusted with much.

Coach's Keys

 What are some of the little things that you do well?

 In what areas could you improve on the little things?

 Will you trust God that he has given you what you need? And that he will give you more if he believes you're ready for it?

Chapter 9

Why

*Now if life is to be complete, we must move
beyond our self-interest. We must move beyond
humanity and reach up, way up for the God of
the universe, whose purpose changeth not.*

—Martin Luther King Jr.

I believe all coaches need to ask themselves this
question. Why am I doing what I'm doing? Why
am I in the coaching business? I believe that coaches
should ask themselves this question more than once.
Some difficult seasons might make you ask it to your-

self every week. We all need to be prepared to answer this question at any given moment.

Here's the deal. Seventy percent of coaches will say they love to work with players and "make a difference." Twenty percent of coaches will tell you they love hoops and they always wanted to get into coaching, and the other ten percent of coaches will just try to tell you what they think they want to hear (all theoretical percentages). But here is my "good, bad, and the ugly" primary reasons why men/women are in the coaching world.

1) They really do love basketball. They think about it all the time. They talk about it, watch it, listen to it, and find ways to learn more about it.

2) They don't have many other skills or aspirations outside of basketball. Many players get finished playing and don't have a whole lot of direction as to what career path they might take, and coaching just seems like it's the natural next step or the only next step.

3) They want to be famous and bask in the glory of being a champion. Many folks want to become a head coach so they can control the program, they can be at the

press conference, they can be well-known and highly regarded.

4) They love working with young people. They enjoy helping young people grow and develop and improve. These coaches will push players in academics and on the court. These coaches are not looking for their own glory; they want to see their players grow and get recognized.

5) There is a ton of money at the highest levels of basketball, and it's a fun business to be in. These coaches understand how the business side of the game works, and they are making their plans to work their way up to make a great living through the game.

Now I'm sure there are some other reasons why coaches are in the game, but these are some of the glaring reasons why people jump into coaching. But I think it is essential that we ask ourselves what our *why* is as a coach. This will give us direction and clarity on who we want to be as a coach, and it sets a level of realistic expectations.

For instance, if coaches are saying they really just want to impact the youth and make a difference, yet they are frustrated with the lack of pay, the difficulty of parents, and the fact that they haven't been recognized for all their efforts…then their *why* doesn't match up with their expectations. Making an impact on players doesn't have anything to do with money or compensation. In fact, I would argue that most of the coaches that make the greatest impact receive the lowest compensation for coaching.

Or if a coach has stated that they are looking for more meaningful relationships throughout the game and wish they had more time to impact players, yet they are in the game at a high level, where everyone is judged based upon performance day in and day out, week in and week out, year in and year out. This coach will likely be let down by the often shifting in staff and players and possible lack of depth in relationships. The more winning, the less shifting, however. That's how the business goes.

So our why is huge. And it's up to you. No one can tell you why you do it or want to do it. Just know, if you are confused on your why, then you'll find yourself questioning a lot without clarity on how you want to move forward. We've got to lock into our why. It will help us be the leaders that we are called to be as coaches.

While it is important to know what our *why* is, it is even more important for us to know what our players' *why* is. Players have all kinds of reasons for playing the game. Here are several that I've compiled…I do understand this is not a sufficient list.

1) Their parents want them to.
2) They want a scholarship to play in college.
3) They need a scholarship or else they can't go to college.
4) They want to play in front of big crowds and hit big shots.
5) Girls like athletes.
6) They'll get more followers on social media.
7) They want to play in the NBA.
8) They want to make a truckload of money so they can buy a ridiculous sized house that they only live in for three months out of a year and with luxury cars in the garage and a huge closet that is dedicated to their shoe game.
9) They just love it. They would do it every day, all the time if they could. They love to compete and the game brings them satisfaction. And they want to be the best they can be. Maybe even the best to ever play.
10) They understand that they have a talent that can eventually open up more doors for them down the road.

As I said, I do understand this list is not truly telling of why all players play. However, if we can know the why of our players, then we will know best on how to motivate them. And the true difficulty is each player has a different why—even at the highest levels. If we can tap into that, then we'll have a better idea on how to communicate with them day in and day out and how we can get the best out of them.

Our why is everything, and it gives us purpose and direction as a coach. And no matter what level you are coaching in—youth, high school, college or pro—if you are a Christian, then your why has to go deeper.

So let's look at God's *why*. Why did he send his son to earth and ultimately the cross? Why does he coach us with discipline and grace that seems to be unending? Let's look into his word.

If you are a Christian, then this is probably one of the first verses you memorized as a child…

> For God so loved the world that he gave his one and only son, that whoever believes in him shall not perish but have eternal life. For God did not send his son into the world to condemn

the world but to save the world through him. Whoever believes in him is not condemned, but whoever does not believe stands condemned already because he has not believed in the name of God's one and only son. (John 3:16–18)

These are Jesus's words. In this passage he is talking to a man named Nicodemus who was a part of the Jewish religious council called the Pharisees. Nicodemus had several questions for Jesus after he had heard his teaching and had seen many of his miracles. In this passage Jesus is basically laying out the Gospel (the word Gospel itself means "Truth"). Here is my attempt to sum up the Gospel...

1) God created man in his own image, and he created man to be in relationship with God.
2) Man (Adam and Eve) caused a fracture in this pure and seamless relationship between man and God when they sinned, disobeying God in the Garden of Eden.

3) God is Holy and without blemish, and he cannot have sin in his presence. Therefore, there was an enormous gap between man and God because of sin.

4) From this point forward, people were not living as they were created to live—in constant loving community with their creator. God and his wonderful creation were separated.

5) This is huge, and we must understand this—To be in union with God is to be alive. To be separated from God is to be dead. Paul writes to the church in Rome about this, "For the wages of sin is death, but the gift of God is eternal life in Christ Jesus our Lord" (Rom. 6:23)

6) So in effort to bring man back into a loving relationship with God, our creator sent his sinless son to connect with humanity. Not only was he sent to connect with us, he was sent to redeem us. The penalty for sin is death, and Christ came to pay our penalty. He chose to do this so that we could be reunited with our God who created us. Jesus's death on the cross, taking our place for the punishment that we deserve is the

"gift of God" that Paul is speaking about in Romans 6:23.

7) Let's go back to the scripture above. In John 3, Jesus himself was telling Nicodemus that if we would believe in him as the Son of God and accept his gift of dying for us in our place, then we will not be condemned. But if we reject his gift, then there is no way we can be unified with our creator again. And remember, separation from God is death in itself. Christ Jesus is the only way because he is God in human form, and if we reject Jesus, then we reject God the father.

8) Now comes this awesome part. Our God is not a transactional God. Once we have been redeemed and brought back into community with our God, our true life has begun. It's not a box that we check and just move on. After we are brought back to God, his *why* really kicks in. He doesn't just want us to be a part of a religion; he wants us to be like his son. So now, his purpose with us is making us more like Jesus because Jesus is the human who is in deepest union with God. And because he loves us so much, he

wants to have that close union with us as well.

9) This is why he coaches us. This is why he disciplines, corrects, encourages, and strengthens us. This is why he gives us grace when we slip up and drift from him. It's because he wants to be in constant union with us. He wants us to be what he created us to be—people who are living full of life and connected to our God where sin has no power in our lives. He wants us to be like him.

10) And that is the Gospel. The truth about our God and us is in a nutshell. His why is earth-shattering, death-conquering, and people-saving.

If you've already believed in Jesus as the son of God and accepted his gift of salvation through his death and resurrection, then you are a part of the family of God, never to be completely separated from him again.

If you have not ever accepted Jesus as who he claims to be, then I encourage you to see if there is more to life than what you've experienced. Would you ask the question of why you are here? Would you pray to God and see what he tells you is true? Would you accept his gift and join me and so many others on the pursuit of becoming more like Jesus? I sure hope so. It would be an honor to have you as part of this team of coaches who are pursuing God and making players and the game better with the love of God.

COACH's KEYS

 So why do you coach? I mean, deep down, why do you coach?

 What is God's deeper purpose with you being in the coaching field?

 How can you help your players or those you influence understand their purpose in what they're doing?

Conclusion

Throughout my time as a player, I had faith in myself, and I believed I could play at a high level in college even if I was alone in my thinking. Looking back, some of it was naivety, and some of it was just pride in the work that I had put in. I had faith in my basketball ability, but I also had faith in my God. Now I don't believe God just gives us whatever we want. But I do believe if we pursue him and chose to honor him over ourselves, then he will also bless us with gifts that only he can give. Psalm 37:4 says, "Delight yourself in the Lord, and he will give you the desires of your heart." And if we truly delight ourselves in the Lord, then what we desire will begin to line up with what he desires. Through all of this, I certainly had some ups and downs spiritually, but my faith in Jesus has withstood the challenges. God calls us to have faith even if it's a bit naïve. No, *only* if it's a bit naïve! We can't calculate and plan and make sense of everything. We don't know God's plan, and he doesn't ask us to figure it all out. He asks us to stay close to him and have faith.

The truth is he doesn't only call us into faith, but he calls us to fight! We can't just lay down when things don't go our way. If we truly believe in something, then we don't just give in and change our stance when it gets challenged. There is truly no faith without fight. And as we read the Word, we see this is lived out in Jesus's life. He fought for us to the death, and in his death he actually redeemed us to be closer to him than we ever could have been otherwise. And he didn't just fight for us two thousand years ago when the world executed him for being different than them, being without sin. He fought for us then, and he fights for us now. And why? Because he has faith. He doesn't get bogged down in who you are *not*. He knows who his father created you to be; and he knows that you can't be the incredible coach, spouse, parent, or friend that he originally intended for you to be *unless* you are in relationship with him. Our God has faith in us. He has faith in you!

Keep the faith. Stay in the fight!

About the Author

Colin Stevens is the founder and CEO of Manzer Basketball Academy and F2 Basketball. His background ranges from playing Division 1 NCAA basketball to climbing the corporate ranks in banking. In 2009, he started Manzer with the focus on developing talent on and off the court. Growing the business by changing lives and pushing athletic results has attracted higher level players and coaches to the program since its inception. In 2016, F2 Basketball was developed to cater to the professional player and high level college players, coaches, and agents. Today, F2 trains talent for the NBA, NCAA, and European leagues.

Stevens built his team around two core principles that drive his companies to success—high level basketball training and God. His tough training disposition is rooted deeply in his passion for Christ. Be it working in the gym, doing reps on the court, or coaching in life, Stevens aims to keep his faith in the forefront without compromise.

His role as a father and husband travels with him. He is devoted to inspire a better life to all of those around him. Be it as a guest preacher at his church, speaking to professional business owners or just talking with his family during dinner, he desires to connect in an authentic and genuine manner.

His first book is a part of his legacy. It is important because it is anchored by God's word. It is the doorway that will allow you to see the future he has in spreading the Word, basketball, and business.

CPSIA information can be obtained
at www.ICGtesting.com
Printed in the USA
LVHW091250160719
624266LV00001B/1/P